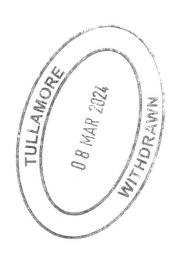

In the Picture With

Mary Cassatt

By Iain Zaczek

WAYLAND

WAYLAND

This edition published in 2014 by Wayland

Copyright © 2014 Brown Bear Books Ltd.

Wayland
Hachette Children's Books
338 Euston Road
London NW1 3BH

Wayland Australia
Level 17/207 Kent Street
Sydney, NSW 2000

All Rights Reserved.

Brown Bear Books Ltd.
First Floor
9–17 St. Albans Place
London
N1 0NX

Author: Iain Zaczek
Managing Editor: Tim Cooke
Designer and artwork: Supriya Sahai
Picture Manager: Sophie Mortimer
Design Manager: Keith Davis
Editorial director: Lindsey Lowe
Children's publisher: Anne O'Daly

ISBN–13: 978-0-7502-8456-1

Printed in China

10 9 8 7 6 5 4 3 2 1

Wayland is a division of Hachette Children's Books,
an Hachette UK company.
www.hachette.co.uk

Picture credits
Key: b = bottom, bgr = background, c = centre, is = insert,
l = left, mtg = montage, r = right, t = top.

Special thanks to The Art Archive
Front Cover, ©The Art Archive/National Gallery of Art
Washington/Superstock; FC t©Public Domain/Foundation of
American Art: 4, ©Public Domain/National Portrait Gallery
Washington; 5tr, ©Library of Congress; 6cl, ©Public Domain/
Walters Art Museum; 6br, ©The Art Archive/National Gallery;
7, ©Public Domain/Deutsches Historischs Museum: 8,
©Public Domain/Metropolitan Museum of Art/Edouard
Baldus; 9t, ©Public Domain/Laird & Lee Chicago; 10-11,
©The Art Archive/Ashmolean Museum; 11, ©The Art Archive/
DeA Picture Library/G. Nimatallah; 12-13, ©The Art Archive/
Musee d'Orsay/Superstock; 15, ©The Art Archive/DeA Picture
Library; 17, ©The Art Archive/DeA Picture Library; 19, ©The
Art Archive/Superstock; 21, ©The Art Archive/Superstock;
22-23, ©The Art Archive/National Gallery of Art Washington/
Superstock; 24-25, ©The Art Archive/Philadelphia Museum of
Art/Superstock; 26-27, ©Public Domain/Metropolitan Museum
of Art; 27, ©The Tate Gallery.

All artwork: © Brown Bear Books

Brown Bear Books has made every attempt to contact the
copyright holder. If you have any information please contact
licensing@brownbearbooks.co.uk

Contents

Life story

Mary Cassatt was an important artist. She was a woman painter at a time when most famous painters were men, and she was an American who lived and worked in France.

Mary Stevenson Cassatt was born on 22 May, 1844, in Allegheny City, Pennsylvania. Her parents were wealthy. Her father, Robert Cassatt, was a banker. He also became mayor of Allegheny City. His family had originally come from France to America in the 17th century. Mary's mother, Katherine, loved the arts and reading books.

Birth name: **Mary Stevenson Cassatt**

Born: **22 May, 1844, Allegheny City, Pittsburgh, Pennsylvania, United States**

Died: **14 June, 1926, near Paris, France**

Nationality: **American**

Field: **Painting, printmaking**

Movement: **Impressionism**

Influenced by: **Impressionism, Edgar Degas, Édouard Manet, Gustave Courbet, Japanese printmaking**

Mary Cassatt
Edgar Degas (c.1880)

Move to Europe

In 1851 the Cassatt family moved to Europe. They lived in France and then in Germany. Mary learned to speak French and German. She enjoyed the European lifestyle. In 1855 the Cassatts returned to the United States. On the way back, they stopped in Paris. They saw an exhibition of paintings by French artists such as Ingres, Delacroix, Degas and Pissarro.

Art classes

In 1861 Mary joined an art class at the Pennsylvania Academy of Fine Arts, in Philadelphia. It was not unusual for a woman to be interested in art, but in 1865 Mary made a decision that was very unusual. She decided to study art in Europe. Her family tried to stop her, but Mary was determined to go. In 1866 Mary and her mother returned to Paris.

Famous Paintings:

- **Young Woman Sewing in a Garden** 1880–1882
- **At the Opéra** 1879
- **The Child's Bath** 1893
- **The Boating Party** 1893–1894
- **'Set of Ten' Prints** 1890–1891

'If painting is no longer needed, it seems a pity that some of us are born into the world with such a passion for line and colour.'

5

WOMEN AT WORK

Before Mary, two other American women had moved to Europe to become artists. In 1853 Harriet Hosmer went to Rome, Italy. She became a sculptor. Edmonia Lewis also studied sculpture in Rome. In 1868, U.S. President Ulysses S. Grant asked her to make a stone portrait of his head.

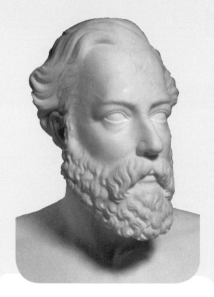

Edmonia Lewis also made this bust of Dio Lewis, a famous American doctor, in 1868.

Exciting city

Paris was an exciting city. It attracted many artists. Most painted traditional subjects, but there were also many who were trying new ideas. An artist named Édouard Manet was painting scenes of everyday life. Other artists were also trying new ways of painting.

Mary had lessons in art. At first she copied old pictures in galleries and museums. This was how many artists learned to paint. She also picked up some new ideas. In 1868 she had a painting accepted by the Paris Salon. This was an exhibition of the best paintings in France. In 1870 France went to war with its neighbour, Prussia (now part of Germany). Mary moved back to Philadelphia until the war was over.

A new home

In 1874, after travelling and painting in Italy and Spain, Mary decided to settle in Paris. The decision changed her life. The same year a group of young artists staged their own exhibition there. These artists were named the 'Impressionists'. They wanted to paint things as they really looked.

OLD MASTERS

In Italy and Spain, Mary studied the works of great painters, such as the Spanish artist Goya. Goya painted Doña Isabel de Porcel in 1805.

FRANCE AT WAR
The Franco-Prussian War interrupted Mary's studies in Paris. She returned to the United States until it was over.

Mary was excited by their methods. She began using paler colours and painting outdoors, which was unusual. She made important new friends. One was an American art collector named Louisine Waldron Elder (later Havemeyer). Mary persuaded her to buy pictures painted by the Impressionists.

Mary's own paintings were beginning to attract attention from the Impressionists. When Degas saw one of her paintings he said, 'There is someone who feels as I do.' Mary met Degas in 1877. They became friends. Degas asked Mary to exhibit her paintings with the Impressionists. For the first time, Mary felt she could paint what she liked. She did not have to worry about the judges at the Paris Salon.

Important people

Edgar Degas – friend, artist

Katherine Kelso Cassatt – mother

Édouard Manet – friend, artist

Louisine Havemeyer – friend, art collector

'I hated conventional art. I began to live.'

Mary's paintings were included in four Impressionist exhibitions. She was becoming famous. Her pictures were often paintings of people. She painted members of her own family when they visited Paris.

Growing fame

In the 1890s Mary worked hard. She began to make prints as well as paintings. She created designs that could be copied many times. Now, she became famous in the United States. In 1892 she was asked to paint a mural for the 'Women's Building' at the 1893 World's Columbian Exposition in Chicago. Mary painted a huge 15-metre-long (50-ft) work called *Modern Woman*.

Mary was now wealthy enough to buy the 17th-century Château de Beaufresne outside Paris. It became her summer home.

The Impressionists

The Impressionists held their first exhibition in Paris in 1874. They were a group of young artists who wanted to paint in a new way. The Impressionists often painted outside. They tried to paint things as they really looked.

Mary lived in Paris for nearly 50 years. The city was famous for its artists. Many of the world's best painters lived there.

The Women's Building at the World's Columbian Exposition in Chicago where Mary painted her huge mural *Modern Woman.*

In 1895 Mary's mother died. Mary went back to visit her family in the United States for the first time in 25 years, but she soon returned to France.

Mothers and babies

In the 1900s Mary spent a lot of time with Louisine. Mary advised Louisine and her husband on what paintings to buy for their art collection. Mary was also asked to paint portraits of mothers and their children. This subject had become her speciality. In 1904 the French government awarded her the Légion d'Honneur medal for services to art.

By 1910 Mary was becoming ill. She could not paint much any more. Her eyesight was failing. Mary died at the Château de Beaufresne in June 1926.

Important places

Allegheny City – Pennsylvania
Pittsburgh – Pennsylvania
Parma – Italy
Seville – Spain
Paris – France
Chicago – Illinois

Cézanne doesn't believe that everyone should see alike.

How Cassatt painted

Mary began painting in a traditional way. Later she was influenced by the Impressionists and by Japanese printmakers.

At the start of her career, Mary travelled widely and studied the work of painters from the past. She particularly liked the work of the Spaniard Diego Velázquez (1599–1660) and the Flemish artist Peter Paul Rubens (1577–1640).

In 1877, Mary met the Impressionist Edgar Degas. Mary began to paint scenes from modern, everyday life. She often painted outdoors.

Japanese prints

Mary liked the style of Japanese artists. They made prints that could be copied on a printing press. The shapes seem simple, but the sizes of things in this landscape by the artist Hiroshige do not seem lifelike. This boat looks a little too big compared to the shore.

Like Degas, Mary painted everyday scenes. Degas used unusual angles, like this view of a woman's back.

At the Milliner's
Edgar Degas (1883)

Her painting style and choice of subjects were like that of Manet and Degas.

In the 1880s Mary changed her style again. She became known for her portraits of women and children. In the 1890s, she began to make prints. She had been inspired by Japanese woodblock prints and 'drypoint' engraving. Mary's paintings changed, too. Her figures appear more solid, and have clear outlines. She also began to use bold colours.

Important French Painters

Paul Cézanne
Gustave Courbet
Edgar Degas
Édouard Manet
Jean-François Millet
Claude Monet
Camille Pissarro
Pierre-Auguste Renoir

Young Woman Sewing in a Garden

Mary painted this picture between 1880 and 1882. It is in the style of the Impressionists. The painting was shown in the last exhibition by the Impressionists in 1886.

Mary's painting was unusual. The girl is at the front of the picture, so she looks big. There isn't room to fit her whole dress into the painting. Her position is straight and upright, like the tree behind her. This makes the girl stand out from the swirling background. The slanting path gives the picture a feeling of space or distance.

The girl looks serious. Her face is drawn in detail. The plants behind her are more like impressions of flowers and trees.

In the Frame

🌱 The original painting of *Young Woman Sewing in a Garden* is 92 cm (36 in) tall and 65 cm (25.5 in) wide.

🌱 Cassatt often painted images of women and children in everyday settings.

🌱 The painting was done in oil on canvas.

CASSATT'S

Palette of the picture

The edges of the girl's skirt are blurred. This style of painting was popular with the Impressionists.

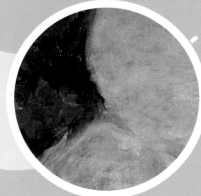

Mary only sketches in the shape of the chair the girl sits on. It does not look very solid.

Mary liked her models to wear white clothing. It could reflect nearby colours. That made it more interesting to paint.

At the Opéra

Mary painted this picture of a woman at the theatre in Paris in 1879. The theatre was a popular subject for Impressionist artists. Degas and Renoir both painted scenes in theatres.

The woman is attending a matinee, or afternoon performance. It is the interval, so the theatre lights are on. The woman is not looking down at the stage. She is looking through her opera glasses (small binoculars) at other people in the audience. She does not know that a man in another box is looking at her. Matinees had been introduced in 1869. They were popular with women.

The other people at the theatre are only shown as shapes. There is no detail in their faces.

I am independent! I can live alone and I love to work.

In the Frame

🎨 The original painting of *At the Opéra* is 81 cm (31.9 inches) tall and 66 cm (26 inches) wide.

🎨 The model for the picture was Mary's sister, Lydia.

🎨 The original painting is in the Museum of Fine Arts, Boston, USA.

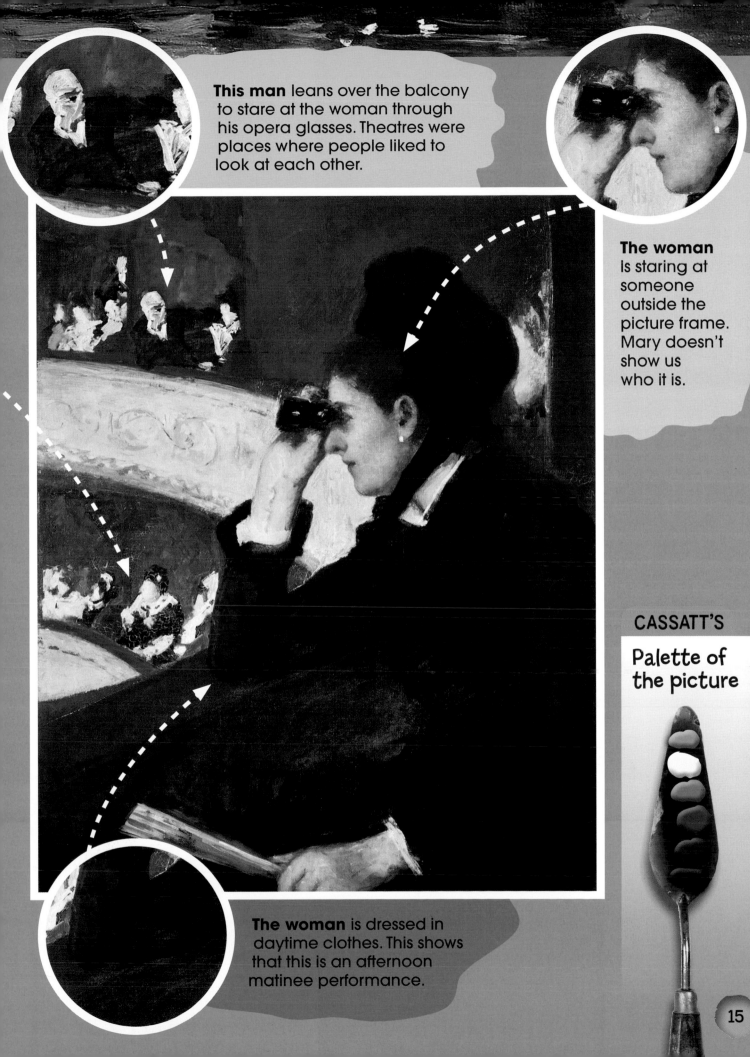

This man leans over the balcony to stare at the woman through his opera glasses. Theatres were places where people liked to look at each other.

The woman Is staring at someone outside the picture frame. Mary doesn't show us who it is.

CASSATT'S

Palette of the picture

The woman is dressed in daytime clothes. This shows that this is an afternoon matinee performance.

The Child's Bath

Mary painted this picture in 1893. A few years earlier she had visited a major exhibition of Japanese prints in Paris. The prints gave her some ideas to use in her own paintings.

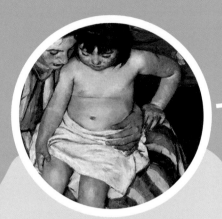

Mary was skilled at painting children in natural poses, or positions. The little girl supports herself on the woman's knee.

Mary's picture uses an unusual viewpoint, or angle. We are looking down on the woman and child. The figures have strong, clear shapes and outlines. The woman could be the mother of the little girl, but children in wealthy families were often bathed by a maid. However, by the 1880s mothers began to spend more time with their children.

CASSATT'S

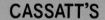

Palette of the picture

In the Frame

🖌 The original painting of *The Child's Bath* is 100 cm (39.5 inches) tall and 66 cm (26 inches) wide.

🖌 Mary often painted children and their parents or nursemaids.

🖌 The original painting is in the Art Institute of Chicago, USA.

The two figures are looking down. That takes our eyes down to the main part of the picture.

Mary liked to paint her figures at the front of pictures. They often seem huge. This woman only just fits into the frame.

Mary used different angles in her pictures. The top of the jug is seen from slightly above, but the pattern is seen from the side.

The Letter

Mary's inspiration for this picture is clear. This woman could easily be Japanese.

Mary's most unusual pictures were her prints. This print comes from a series of colour prints known as the 'Set of Ten'. They are Mary's most famous prints. She exhibited them together in 1891.

Mary's prints were based on Japanese prints she had seen. She also used ideas from her friend Edgar Degas, who was also a good printmaker. To make a print, Mary scratched a picture on a plate of copper. She added ink to the surface. Then she pressed paper against the plate to make the print. Mary used a technique called aquatint to add colour. She coated parts of the copper plate with coloured powder as well as ink. It gave more variety to the print.

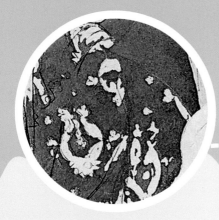

Mary loved the colours and decoration of Japanese prints. She spent a lot of time on the detail of the pattern on the woman's dress.

CASSATT'S

Palette of the picture

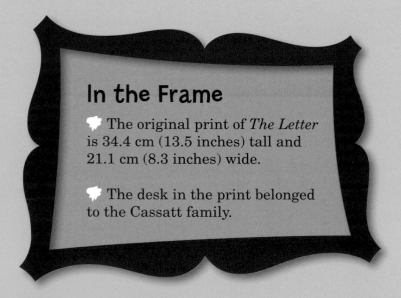

In the Frame

🍂 The original print of *The Letter* is 34.4 cm (13.5 inches) tall and 21.1 cm (8.3 inches) wide.

🍂 The desk in the print belonged to the Cassatt family.

This detail would have seemed modern to Mary's audience. Envelopes sealed with sticky gum were quite new at the time.

The edges of the writing surface are at different angles. Mary used the Japanese technique of showing the same object from different viewpoints.

19

In the Omnibus

The mother's face is drawn with bold, black outlines.

This image shows passengers in a horse-drawn omnibus, or bus. It is another print from the 'Set of Ten' from 1891. In her first drawings of the scene, Mary included a man and another woman. She decided to leave them out and just show this small group.

Mary is famous for her pictures of mothers and children. Here the child's mother looks out of the window at the river while a nanny looks after the child. The dark, straight lines on the women's dresses are made with a technique called drypoint. The bigger coloured areas on the dresses are created with aquatint.

Mary liked to show details from everyday life. This type of baby clothing was worn by both boys and girls. It is very smart.

In the Frame

🍂 The original print of *In the Omnibus* is 36.8 cm (14.5 inches) tall and 26 cm (10.5 inches) wide.

🍂 Mary printed 25 copies of the finished picture.

There are two ways for a painter: the broad and easy one or the narrow and hard one.

This is a bridge over the River Seine, in the centre of Paris. Mary usually painted women in their homes.

This woman's hat is much smaller than the other woman's. This means she is probably the child's nanny.

CASSATT'S

Palette of the picture

The Boating Party

Mary painted this picture in 1893 or 1894 while she was on holiday in the south of France. The bright colours and lack of shadows suggest the strong Mediterranean sunlight.

Mary probably got the idea for this subject from *Boating*, a painting by Édouard Manet. Manet was one of her favourite artists. Mary told her friends, the Havemeyers, that they should buy his picture. She told them it was 'the last word in painting', meaning that it was the best. The design of Mary's own picture is bold and lifelike.

In the Frame

🍃 The original painting of *The Boating Party* is 90.2 cm (35.5 inches) tall and 117.5 cm (46.25 inches) wide.

🍃 Mary included the painting in her first major U.S. exhibition in 1895.

Mary paints from a very low angle. She cuts the boat off at the frame to make the viewer feel like a passenger in the boat.

The horizon line at the top of the picture helps to bring our eyes to the woman in the boat.

The woman and child look at the rower. Is this a family outing, or is the rower a hired boatman?

CASSATT'S

Palette of the picture

Mary did not often paint men. At the time, a woman artist would not have been allowed to be alone with a male model in the studio.

Family Group Reading

Mary painted this picture in 1898. It was bought by her friend Louisine Havemeyer. They had met in Paris when Louisine was a young student. Louisine later married a wealthy businessman.

Mary taught Louisine about art. She helped the Havemeyers build up a large art collection. Louisine eventually owned many paintings by Monet, Manet, and Degas. She also owned 20 of Mary's works.

Louisine helped bring Impressionist paintings to the United States. Images of women and children reading were popular at the time.

CASSATT'S

Palette of the picture

In the Frame

The original painting of *Family Group Reading* is 56.5 cm (22.25 inches) tall and 112.4 cm (44.25 inches) wide.

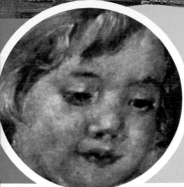

Mary was good at painting children. She said: 'I love to paint children. They are so natural and truthful.'

The mother's face is painted with great attention to detail.

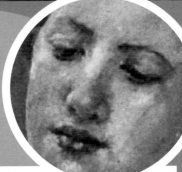

The girl rests both her hands on her mother's, as she holds the book open.

The sky can only really be seen reflected in the water.

What came next?

Mary Cassatt helped to make Impressionism popular, especially in the United States. She also helped to make it more acceptable for women to be artists.

There were not many female Impressionist painters. Like her male friends, Mary wanted to paint scenes from everyday life. The male Impressionists often painted in bars and cafés in Paris. A woman could not go to such places without causing outrage. Instead, Mary chose to paint the lives of women like herself. Her paintings show people going to the theatre, driving a carriage, having fittings with a dressmaker, taking care of their children or visiting friends.

Famous Women Artists

- Sonia Delaunay
- Gwen John
- Frida Kahlo
- Tamara de Lempicka
- Margaret MacDonald
- Berthe Morisot
- Georgia O'Keeffe
- Suzanne Valadon

AFTER MARY'S CAREER, it was easier for women to become artists. The Welsh painter Gwen John spent most of her life working in France.

Gwen John
Young Woman Holding
a Black Cat, c.1920.

Mary also helped to make the work of the Impressionists popular. The Cassatts were wealthy, so Mary knew other wealthy Americans. She persuaded them to buy her friends' paintings and leave them to museums in their wills. This helped the Impressionists sell more pictures at higher prices. Many members of the group made enough money to live on.

Mary also helped other women artists. In 1893 she was asked to create a huge mural, or wall-painting, for the World's Columbian Exposition in Chicago. This was an important international art exhibition. Mary's mural decorated the Women's Building, and she chose a subject that summed up her own life and work: *Modern Woman*.

FREDERICK CHILDE HASSAM was another American Impressionist. Like Mary, he helped to make Impressionism popular outside Europe.

Childe Hassam
Celia Thaxter's Garden, 1890.

How to paint like Cassatt

Painting exactly like Mary is very hard. She trained at art school for years. But it is still fun to try painting the same kinds of subjects that Mary enjoyed painting.

WHAT YOU'LL NEED:

- a photograph (to copy)

- a pencil

- thick white paper or card

- coloured crayons

- small brushes

- acrylic paints

1.

Find a photograph to copy. Perhaps it could be of you and your mum or dad when you were little, or of you and your brothers and sisters.

2.

Using a pencil, lightly sketch the shapes from the photograph onto a piece of stiff white paper or card.

3.

Outline the shapes of your drawing with coloured crayons. This was a technique Mary used when she made prints. Do not worry if the lines are not completely clear. You can go over the same part again and again until it looks right.

4.

Use paints to fill in the colour and detail of your drawing. Mary liked lighter colours. She also knew that you don't have to fill in every detail. If you prefer, leave parts of the picture such as the background so they are quite sketchy. This will make them look more Impressionistic, like the paintings of Mary's friends.

Timeline

- **1844:** Born in Allegheny City, Pennsylvania, USA.
- **1851:** Moves to Europe for four years.
- **1861:** Studies at the Pennsylvania Academy of Fine Arts in Philadelphia.
- **1866:** Moves to Paris to study art.
- **1870:** Leaves Paris because of the Franco–Prussian War.
- **1873:** Returns to settle in Paris.
- **1877:** Meets Edgar Degas, who introduces her to the Impressionists.
- **1879:** Exhibits paintings at the Impressionists' exhibition.
- **1892:** Paints *Modern Woman* for an international exhibition in Chicago.
- **1926:** Dies after a long illness.

Glossary

aquatint: A form of printing that uses coloured powder to create different effects.

drypoint engraving: A form of printing in which the artist scratches lines into a wax covering on a metal plate to create a picture.

etching: A design made by scratching a drawing on a metal plate.

mural: A large painting that is painted directly onto a wall or another surface.

palette: The range of colours an artist uses in a particular painting or group of paintings.

plate: A flat piece of copper or other metal on which a design is drawn in order to create a print.

print: An image that is drawn on a sheet of metal or other material so that it can be covered in ink and pressed onto a sheet of paper to produce a picture.

sketch: A rough drawing that is often done in preparation for making a larger painting.

traditional: Something that has been done in the same way for a long time.

viewpoint: The position in which someone stands to see a particular scene.

Further information

BOOKS

Baby Loves. Metropolitan Museum of Art. Atheneum, 2003.

Mattern, Joanne. *Mary Cassatt* (Great Artists). Checkerboard Library, 2005.

Casey, Carolyn. *Mary Cassatt: The Life of an Artist* (Artist Biographies). Enslow Publishers Inc, 2004.

Hoena, Blake A. *Mary Cassatt* (Masterpieces: Artists and their Works). Bridgestone Books, 2003.

O'Connor, Jane. *Mary Cassatt: Family Pictures* (Smart ABout Art). Turtleback, 2003.

Harris, Lois. *Mary Cassatt: Impressionist Painter*. Pelican Publishing, 2007.

Merberg, Julie. *Quiet Time with Cassatt* (Mini Masters). Chronicle Books, 2006.

MUSEUMS

You can see Mary's famous paintings from this book in these museums:

Young Woman Sewing in a Garden
Musée d'Orsay, Paris, France.

At the Opéra
Museum of Fine Arts, Boston, USA.

The Child's Bath
Art Institute of Chicago, USA.

The Letter
There are numerous copies of this print. One is in the Worcester Art Museum, Worcester, Massachusetts, USA.

In the Omnibus
There are numerous copies of this print. One is in the National Gallery of Art, Washington, DC, USA.

The Boating Party
National Gallery of Art, Washington, DC, USA.

Family Group Reading
Philadelphia Museum of Art, USA.

WEBSITES

www.nga.gov/kids/scoop-cassatt.pdf
A pull-out about Mary from the National Gallery of Art in Washington.

www.marycassatt.org
An online gallery of all of Mary's works.

makingartfun.com/htm/f-maf-art-library/mary-cassatt-biography.htm
'Hey Kids, Meet Mary Cassatt,' from Making Art Fun.

totallyhistory.com/mary-cassatt/
A biography of Mary on the Totally History website.

Index